CHURCH PROJECT

A Biblical, Simple, and Relevant Pursuit of Church

JASON SHEPPERD

LUCIDBOOKS

First Printing 2017

ISBN-10: 1632961091
ISBN-13: 9781632961099
eISBN-10: 1632961105
eISBN-13: 9781632961105

TABLE OF CONTENTS

Acknowledgments...v
A Note to Pastors..ix

Chapter One: The Church Project Story...............................1

Chapter Two: The Three Pillars of
a New Testament Church...13
    Sunday Gatherings..15
    House Churches...20
    Ministry Partnerships..22

Chapter Three: Guiding Biblical Values............................29
    Unashamedly Biblical...29
    Irreducibly Simple..31
    Understandably Relevant.......................................34
    Radically Generous..35

Chapter Four: Profile of a House Church.........................45
    Biblical Defense of House Church..........................46
    Profile of a House Church.......................................49

Chapter Five: Overview of a House Church Pastor..............61

Role and Responsibility of a House Church Pastor...........63
Raising Up a New Pastor...67

Conclusion...73

Appendix A: 10 Things I'd Tell Church Planters...................79
Appendix B: Things That Have Surprised Me.......................85

ACKNOWLEDGMENTS

WHEN ASKED IF I would ever write a book, I have always said that I would if I had something to write about. Well, I'm grateful to have something to write about now. But I never knew what it would take to get to that point.

I don't know much, but I do know that it takes a lot of people to get here—especially when it comes to writing about the church. I'd like to acknowledge some groups of people who have brought about the life of this church.

I'm grateful for wise counsel who saw things in me before I saw them, and believed in me when I didn't. Thank you to the Williford Family, Rob and Gail Richie, Kyle Vann, Armand Abay, Lee Turner, Larry Allbritton, Chris Zaino, and Jeff Wells. I love you, friends.

I'm grateful for a few guys who risked with me to help begin something out of nothing. I'm grateful for Andy White, David Pham, and Kyle Worsham. Talks about ideas became reality. I love you, guys.

A small group of people came before we began and have stuck it out and transferred Church Project DNA to thousands. I'm grateful for about 40 rebels who risked their time and money and families and reputations to pursue the original essence of church. I love you, unique people.

I serve alongside a group of elders I trust with my life, my family, and this church. I don't lead this church alone. Thank you to Rob Richie, George Booth, Hans Molegraaf, Jason Elliott, and Trace Howard. I love you, elders.

The staff at Church Project is stellar. I love them. We are a team. I trust them, depend on them, and believe in them. We wouldn't exist without these people. I work with people who are my friends. I love you, team.

CP is an incredible church of people who really love Jesus, each other, and their world. Thank you for your patience with me and love for me, and for helping me believe more deeply in the beauty of church. So many faithfully serve Jesus and this church and this world in unselfish ways. You are the reality of church. You are the church that love me and my family, and we love you.

Thank you to my friend and mentor, Larry Allbritton, who helped make this book possible.

Thank you to my brother Matt who is brilliant and has genius thoughts about the church and the kingdom. And, he believes in me. I love you, bro.

I'm so thankful for a rare reality to have lifelong friendships with people inside of the church I pastor. I love you, friends.

A family enjoys the great privilege of being the most intimate part of church planting, and pays the greatest price. I'm grateful for Logan, Emma, Payton, Katelynn, Lauren, Carter, and Ty, for giving me grace even when you didn't know you were, and for being the main reason why I want a church to reveal who Jesus is. I love you, kids.

My wife has endured through the really beautiful moments and the really brutal moments of church. You know the price of planting and pastoring a church more than anyone else.

Acknowledgments

You do things for this church that no one other than Jesus and I will know. Thank you for loving people and Jesus and me so well. I love you, Brooke.

Thank you, Jesus, for allowing me to serve you by serving your church. I love you, Jesus.

A NOTE TO PASTORS

LIKE EVERY PASTOR, there are moments we point back to when we know God was pointing us toward his purpose for our life. It was in college when I sensed God calling me to be a pastor. After wrestling with God for years, I finally obeyed and followed what I sensed him pushing me toward. I began finding my way, learning much, growing much, and facing much frustration and discouragement as I attempted to humbly surrender in obedience. But after 20 years as a pastor, I knew I wasn't giving the majority of my time to God's original call on my life. I was making disciples where God placed me, but it felt like I was only doing a small fraction of what he had planned for me.

I wondered if I could find a place or position in a church that would resemble the church and calling that I read about in the Scriptures—that lit my heart on fire as I read. I became so discouraged with not fulfilling my calling and passions that I thought about leaving the ministry and going to make a lot of money in the marketplace. I felt like I could at least support gospel churches and ministries with the money I made. But, after years of frustration and desperation, I decided to risk it all, and pursue the conviction of church God placed in my heart. To me, it didn't matter if 40 people came (which is where we started), 400, or 4,000—I was going to go after this conviction and desire for church with all I had.

In just six years we went from 4 people to closer to 4,000 (about 3,500 people now call our church home, and over 2,000 attend regularly). We've been able to help plant 16 churches, set up about 40 house churches in our city, have given away millions of dollars (50 percent of our budget outside of our walls, which was our commitment from inception) to gospel-centered ministries in our city and world, and have hundreds of our people leading in intentional, one-on-one discipleship relationships.

All of this has happened with no centralized office. No phone. No receptionist. No administrators. No mailers. No commercials. No marketing. We even started in an obscure location with no drive-by visibility. I had actually lived in our area for over 15 years and never knew our building existed.

We intentionally didn't read the books everyone else was reading or go to the conferences everyone else was attending, since most of the church plants we knew of were struggling or failing. We simply took all we found in the Bible over the years and, along with my decades serving in the church, synthesized it with actual, practical application we believed could work in any context.

The name of our church, Church Project, was actually not intended to be our name, but was just the essence of our church from the outset. I called the church this at the beginning, through conversations with a friend, as I was searching and praying for the right name. But we got traction too quickly before we found another name, and the name "Church Project" sort of stuck. I love that our essence of humility is inherently embedded in our name—we are in pursuit of biblical church, and regularly admit we are far from there. We say weekly that we are a church (and we define that), and that we are a project, "a constant pursuit of becoming what Christ originally intended."

I'm writing this book because I really love the church. Our ecclesiology has produced simple, organic systems and philosophy, much generosity, and much growth, which has caused many pastors to spend time with us over the last several years to learn more about what we're doing. I love talking to them because I love the church, and people who love the church. And I love the church because I love Jesus.

In this book, I'll simply describe what has worked for us and what I've shared that has made a difference for other pastors and their churches. As our name connotes, and I easily admit, I don't think we have it all together. But planting and pastoring this church has been fun, fast, and fruitful. So, I'll share what's happened, humbly praying you'll be encouraged, and think more deeply and differently about the church.

I'll keep this short and sweet. The structure of this book is simple. Chapter 1 tells the story of Church Project in more detail—how we started and where we are now. Chapter 2 describes the three pillars of our church, which we chose because we felt they were obviously the essence of the church in the Scriptures. Chapter 3 describes four values that drive and connect all we do. Chapter 4 delves deep into house churches—why it's a biblical model and how they best function. Chapter 5 discusses the role of pastoral leadership in house churches. And finally, there is an appendix with reflections on leadership and church planting. These are lessons I've learned over the years, offered here in hopes they are of help to you.

Whether you are a church planter or you pastor an already established church, my hope is that this book inspires and equips you as you consider how to shape a biblically-faithful church. We started Church Project to re-think church, by returning to the early church as clearly as we could decipher it. I hope reading this book can help you, as a pastor, assess how you are living out your calling in the local church, evaluate what you are perpetuating or creating, and ensure that the practices you perpetuate align with Scripture. If reading this book can help you think more critically about the most crucial organism on the planet—the church—then I'll be satisfied the time spent writing it was well worth the investment.

Thanks for loving Jesus, for serving his church, and for feeding his sheep. I'm thankful to be in the trenches with so many incredible pastors I know and learn from. I pray you'll be refreshed in the calling we share.

CHAPTER ONE

THE CHURCH PROJECT STORY

Y PART IN Church Project began, in some sense, about 25 years ago, long before the church was a reality. I was in college, sitting in my truck, praying to God about my calling to ministry. I remember asking, "If you are calling me to pursue this, please let me be part of what you originally intended the church to be." It took 20 years of ministry for that prayer to be answered.

I love the churches I've served in the past. The people are precious to me, and I am grateful for fruit and relationships that have lasted decades. But for most of my churches (all but one, actually), I was constrained to serve in contexts I felt did not align with my understanding of Scripture or church philosophy. I served God and the people passionately, even though I was wrestling with God about his plan for my life all along the way. But, I also believe God had many reasons for me to be in those churches for over a decade. He wanted me to pour out my life there and make disciples. He wanted me to grow and mature. And, he wanted to push into me a deeper conviction about what church actually is and isn't, to refine my ecclesiology, and to create an absolute inability to remain in pastoral ministry without rethinking church.

I was a teaching pastor at a large church—one with great facilities, a large campus, a solid reputation, widespread impact, and thousands of incredible people. God was moving there in great ways, and I had a great team to lead. For years, the church leaders and I had discussed the line of succession I would step into whenever the lead pastor (whom I loved and respected deeply—and still do) would retire.

But there was finally a moment when I just said, "I can't keep doing this." I knew it was time. Something deep in my soul, that had held me back all of these years, was gone—it was immediately different. I remember calling my wife and saying, "What I've been wrestling with, the things that have been holding me back, are over. I'm released. I'm done, and I can't do it anymore." That's when I decided to risk everything.

Though I had submitted to God's process of preparation for years, waiting for him to cultivate the timing of his plans for me, until this point God hadn't revealed to me that it was time for me to do something else. The final moments leading up to my decision were spent meditating on a parable I had known for years—the parable of the talents (Matt. 25:14–30). In this story, Jesus expresses God's frustration with somebody who doesn't fully leverage their opportunity, blessing, and gifting. I felt an overwhelming sense of conviction that I wasn't properly or fully stewarding my gifts.

I went to the lead pastor and said, "I need to co-pastor, or I need to leave and go pastor. I have to leverage my calling in more ways than I am now." I knew this conversation would lead to my amicable departure, with the pastor and church's blessing, but without any financial support or sending.

It was, as Bill Hybels calls it, a righteous indignation. It was holy discontent. It was a combination of God finally letting me step into my calling and the fact that I was 35 years old and knew, "If not now, when?" It was this sense that there was more to ministry than what I was currently doing. I felt like it was a step-out-and-take-a-risk kind of moment. I literally could not *not* do it. Honestly, I didn't even consider how risky this move was. Risk wasn't part of the conversation or consideration. I just knew that I had to die trying; and though I might die, I was going to give it all I had. It might not work, but the obedience would be worth it. That was it.

If I hadn't taken this step, I would likely have left vocational ministry as a pastor. I had to either take a leap into my calling, or I had to walk away entirely, because I knew that what I was perpetuating wasn't the fullness of my calling. It wasn't bad, but it wasn't full. It wasn't full because God had called and prepared me for something else. God had set me apart, called me, prepared me, and cultivated me. What I had been doing for much of the last 15 or 20 years was not fully that thing. It was time.

I wanted to make sure I left with honor in every way. If Jesus was leading me to do something, even something like leave a church, I knew it must be done honorably (the same should be true for every decision in my life). My pastor and I talked about what our relationship would be like going forward. We wanted to be on the same page and clear about our expectations. I said my interest would never be to do anything but support the work of that church, and I wanted to start a new culture and DNA, with new people, in a new place. What I said would be what I would do—my yes would be yes. Over time, this would end up being true for both of us. We intentionally continued meeting together monthly to ensure our relationship remained strong. We've since traveled internationally together. We have only ever honored one another.

Calling is more than simply a desire to do something great for God. Calling involves a decision on the part of God that we simply respond to and step into. God anoints pastors for their role. I didn't want to do anything that God wasn't initiating, that didn't originate with him. I wanted his will, his hand, and his anointing on this. Anointing is the *powerful* and *present presence* of God for his *purpose*. He calls us and then appoints us for that role. Our role is to *receive* the calling because it comes from him. We can *request* his anointing, but he is not *required* to give it to us. Once given, we seek to *remain* in that anointing by living a holy life of obedience, or he will *remove* the anointing.

I left my position quickly—just a few weeks after the initial conversation with my pastor—and I immediately went to the mountains alone to think and pray. I prayed for a week, saying, "God, I have no idea what to do. Although I believe you're in this, I have no idea what direction to take." I had no plans, no church name, no direction, no money, no people— nothing. But something more important happened that week: God gave me my first four tasks to do.

Those four things were:

- *Find a place to gather some people for conversational meetings.* I had no idea who those people would be because I knew I would not invite anyone who was a part of my former church.

- *Start looking for a few guys who would be willing to take this risk with me.* I did not yet know anyone who had this in their heart, or who was willing to step into this with me.

- *Put together a board of advisors*—wise, godly men who would not necessarily be a part of this new church with me, but who could counsel me through the process.

- *Begin looking for a place, any place, that we might begin exercising this vision and calling.*

The first thing I did when I got back from the mountains was put together a board of men who were faithful in my life. They were men who had walked with me through the years and knew my calling. I trusted their relationship with Jesus, their love for the church, and their love for me. They had a wide variety of experience and led in different domains. They were, and are, wise, and they have given me courage and counseled me well.

Then, God crossed my path with several guys who wanted to take a risk with me. I didn't know two of them, and the other one was only a casual acquaintance. I ran into the first guy at a wedding in a city three hours away, and I brought up the church I was going to pursue. As it happened, this guy lived in my area but had left a church staff because he was hoping for an opportunity exactly like the one I described, but had no idea how, where, or if it would happen. The second man had helped plant a church, but the church had closed its doors. Somehow, he heard about my plans and contacted me. And, as for the third guy, I literally found his business card in the parking lot on a rainy day. I had met him years before, but had made no relationship or contact with him since. I called him the day I found his card. He had just left a mega-church staff in a distant part of the city and was longing to take a risk as well.

The four of us started having regular meetings together. I treated them like staff meetings, as if we actually worked together and had a church to lead. We would pray, study the Scriptures, define our roles, create tasks, and make plans together. I held them accountable as I would have a regular staff, and I encouraged them as they encouraged me. We planned and prayed together. Even though we had no money and I wasn't paying them, we started leading a church as a staff four months before we had anything like a church. We became a team before we had any people to lead or place to gather— before we had anything, really.

One month after the mountain trip, we had our first of four small gatherings as a church, and somehow about 40 people came to it. The same number showed up to each of our four monthly gatherings, with about 25 repeat attenders. So, by the time we started, we had somewhere around 25 people. We didn't want to be divisive, so we asked people not to invite anybody from a church where they'd previously served or attended. We were committed to avoiding a sizable migration from another church and a large sharing of former DNA. It was a fresh start—a collection of Christians from all throughout the area—with no certain church represented more than another. It was a melting pot of believers willing to dream together. I knew very few of the people who showed up, but the few people I did know are still with us today. In fact, I believe almost all of these original people are still here.

At those first meetings, we talked about what we saw in the Bible, what the local church should look like based upon what we saw in the Scriptures, and how we could apply those ideas to our place and time. I told the church, "I have no idea what church like this looks like here, but we're going to be a group of people who figure it out. I don't know if there'll be 40, 400, or 4,000 people, but it really is, in many ways, a project. We're going to see if we can discover this together." And that's what we would do—invite people to join together in a pursuit of what Christ originally intended church to be.

There was no break between those smaller meetings and our launch as a church. We just started doing church. We started preaching the Word, worshiping together, and discipling our kids on Sundays. Much of what we did was, and is, quite common among many churches. We weren't doing anything earth-shattering. Our uniqueness was what you find in our values—unashamedly biblical, intentionally simple, and understandably relevant. We sang songs, preached the Word, prayed, gave, and enjoyed being together. We did simple things like allowing parents and children to join together for part of the service, which birthed a beautiful practice we still do to this day. We made it so that our kids could hear the voices of their parents sing, take communion together, and give together.

I've heard church planters say, "Let's build a core for a long time, and then we'll start doing Bible studies in a living room and share the vision until people get it." I understand that, and it's not altogether a bad idea. Sometimes, it is the best approach. But almost 80 percent of church plants fail, a failure rate that rivals that of small businesses. Many church planters are starting church the same way, reading the same books, and then wondering why they are getting the same results.

But I wanted to try something different, and start the church like I saw Paul starting churches in the Bible. He immediately started doing what he was called to do: preach the Word. My primary gifts weren't in the areas needed for leading small groups. I'm really not great at that. I needed to start exercising my primary gifts of teaching and leadership. So, we started doing what we would always do in the same way we would always do it—and we do the same things today that we did seven years ago.

God has caused great growth over the years, even though we haven't changed much of anything since the beginning. Our gatherings look the same, our elements look the same, our overall church structure is the same. Even our handouts look the same. We've never done a mailer, a commercial, or marketing. We had no sign for drive-by visibility for the first four years of our church. We met in an obscure warehouse that was set off of the main road. You had to work to find us.

By the end of our first year, we had 100 people. By the end of year two, we had 200 people. Between years two and four, we had 1,000 people. Between years four and six, we had 2,000 people. We didn't know what caused explosive growth, as nothing had changed in our approach to anything. We started with two house churches. By the end of year one, we had about four. Soon, we had eight, and then about forty. Our first-year budget was about $275,000. By year six or seven, we had a budget of roughly four million dollars. We've invested into gospel-centered ministry partnerships and church planting with millions of dollars. We've partnered with 16 other Church Project plants, and other churches beyond Church Project. Tens of thousands of people from all over the world have somehow found our podcast and are listening to it each month. We give God the glory—he did this, and did this for himself, and invited us into what he was doing. We simply followed what we saw in his Word, depending on his power all along the way. This church is what he's done.

People sometimes ask me if I'm surprised at what has happened at Church Project in such a short time. I tell them I don't really think about it like that. I'm excited about what's happened, but I'm not satisfied, so I don't feel surprised. I'm driven and passionate about the dreams he's put in my heart for his church, so I'm always thinking about where he is leading us. I'm no more surprised about our journey than

I would have been if the church hadn't made it. It could have easily have gone either way. But God, in his grace, not only allowed our church to survive, but he caused us to become something that he wants to use for himself. According to the best church-planting practices and plans, we should be failing. And that may be the point. We've tirelessly sought to mimic Jesus and his methods, and we believe that's where the power lies. God was pleased about our efforts to build his church in our city for himself—and he's invited us to be a part of his work.

Some pastors of the largest churches I know, men I deeply respect and continue to learn from, have told me, "Jason, we love what you are doing and how you operate, but we feel like we're stuck and we don't know how to get off the hamster wheel." One successful pastor who has had great influence in my life told me, "If we did this—which I wish we could, and I want to—our church would fall apart."

I understand that. It's hard to imagine big change because many of our systems in the church are deeply rooted. We fear we'll lose people, stop progress, or capsize the ministry if we change. I know the hesitation, but I don't think that's a reason to stay as we are.

When we started, we certainly took a risk, but we believed what we were pursuing was theologically and philosophically accurate. That's why we did it. We wouldn't encourage anyone to go and do what we've done unless they saw that it worked in the early church and that it's working now. It boils down to this: if the approach is biblical, we are all constrained to follow that model, and we should have nothing to fear.

But we may have to take a risk.

My goals for this book are simple. I want to help reimagine church according to the Scriptures, and, in light of the evidence found there, scrutinize church practices that don't actually come from Scripture. From there, I hope to give pastors faith and confidence in the Word of God, and trust that the Spirit of God can grow his church his way. Finally, I pray this book helps the church make disciples more effectively so that Jesus is exalted and the gospel is spread.

NOTES

_____

_____

_____

_____

_____

_____

_____

_____

_____

_____

_____

_____

_____

_____

_____

_____

CHAPTER TWO

THE THREE PILLARS
OF A NEW TESTAMENT
CHURCH

I N OUR EARLY gatherings at Church Project, we were driven
by this question: "What do we see in Scripture about how
Jesus designed the church?" We then worked to mimic
that answer as closely as possible. The point of this chapter is
to tell you what we saw in Scripture and how we've sought to
replicate it.

I've often heard what you may be thinking right now.
*The message doesn't change, but the methods do. Culture has
changed and is different in every place and people.* I agree, but
only partially. The launching of the early church represented
cultures and people groups from all over the world. It was
immediately cross-cultural. Yet, it was consistent in its basis
and structure. As we look at the Scriptures, we find these
same structures in the multi-cultural and multi-national early
church: Sunday gatherings together for the whole corporate

body, house churches for dozens to gather intimately, and ministry opportunities to serve one another and the city.

I've traveled all over the world, and some things are always true. People need the church. They long to gather with other believers. There is power in the large, collective gathering of people, and in the smaller gatherings of people. People may not have buildings, but in every culture people have some form of home. And people are in need, so they have an opportunity to serve one another.

In the Gospels, we know that everything Jesus did was about making disciples. His two basic commands for the apostles were "make disciples" (Matt. 28:18–20) and "feed my sheep" (John 21:17). This is exactly what Jesus did the entire time he was on earth. He was making disciples when he taught people on the mountainside by the thousands. When he lived life together with people by the dozens and one-on-one, he was making disciples as well. And, he was making disciples when he was meeting the needs of others.

We see that the early church followed in his footsteps. They met inside the temple courts by the thousands. They met regularly in houses by the dozens. And they met the various needs of those around them. One of the clearest pictures of what the earliest church was like is found in Acts 2:43–47, which shows all of these pillars at play.

> They devoted themselves to the apostles' teaching and to fellowship, to the breaking of bread and to prayer. Everyone was filled with awe at the many wonders and signs performed by the apostles. All the believers were together and had everything in common. They **sold property and possessions to give to anyone who had need.** Every day they continued to meet together **in the temple courts.** They broke bread **in their homes** and ate

together with glad and sincere hearts, praising God and enjoying the favor of all the people. And the Lord added to their number daily those who were being saved. [Emphasis mine.]

(Acts 2:42-47)

For us, it was that simple. Our church decided to concern ourselves with these three pillars: Sunday morning gatherings of the entire church, house churches of smaller communities, and ministry partnerships with those in need. We began to do these things and only these things, and to turn the flywheel on these pillars.

Sunday Gatherings

Sunday gatherings have been essential to the church since its beginning in the book of Acts. Even before the inception of the church, all throughout the Old Testament, God gathered his people together regularly for worship, prayer, and teaching. God obviously values and enjoys his people gathering as one. Taking our cues from the passages mentioned in the paragraphs below, as well as many others (such as Acts 2:42–47), our gatherings have certain regular components, all done with the aim of making disciples.

1. First, we prioritize a **weekly sermon**. Following Paul's commitment to preach the "whole counsel of God" (Acts 20:27), we are committed to verse-by-verse preaching through whole books of the Bible. We take rare breaks throughout the year to address specific topics or to host a guest speaker, but otherwise we practice expository preaching because we believe it is best suited for disciple-making.

2. We also **sing**. In Colossians 3:16, Paul writes, "Let the word of Christ dwell in you richly, teaching and admonishing one another in all wisdom, singing psalms and hymns and spiritual songs, with thankfulness in your hearts to God." We sing songs that exalt Jesus and proclaim great truths about God. We give care and attention to making sure our songs are biblically and doctrinally rich. We also seek to engage everyone in the singing, rather than them being observers of a concert-like performance. In this way, the church enjoys an experience of unity as believers hear one another singing.

3. A unique facet of our gatherings is a time for **silence**. In contrast to our hurried schedules, we want to give people an opportunity to meditate in silence and hear from God. This practice allows us to model for people a practice we hope will continue throughout their week. We regularly hear from people that this is one of the most meaningful moments of the gathering. These few minutes of guided silence and contemplation allow people to practice essential aspects of discipleship—prayer, worship, confession, and repentance.

4. Our gatherings are also marked by **prayer**. When we see God's people meeting together in the New Testament, we usually see them praying (e.g., Acts 2:43ff, 4:29ff, 7:59–60, 9:36–42). At Church Project, we want to commune with God in prayer in various ways throughout the Sunday Gathering, so we pray through singing, through silence, and through Scripture. We have people pray through meditation

as the service begins. We pray during communion by encouraging people to spend moments alone in prayer before receiving the elements. We have moments of silence during songs and between songs when we want our people to pray. Before the sermon, we ask people to prepare their hearts by asking God to speak to them and telling God that they want to hear from him.

5. An essential aspect of this time of prayer happens at the end of every sermon when we have a time of prayerful **reflection** on each major point that we taught through that day. If there are five main ideas in the passage, we ask our people to consider each one of those—confessing their sin and making decisions to obey. We also have pillows at the front of the room where people can kneel and pray on their own. Finally, we have a prayer room where people can go to be prayed for by others in our church or to discuss questions they may have about the gospel. Each of these steps have allowed us to integrate more prayer into our Sunday gatherings.

6. As I previously mentioned, **communion** plays a central role in our Sunday gatherings. We approach this practice in different ways because Scripture gives us the liberty to do so. Weekly, we have response tables around the room where people can take communion on their own, and monthly we have communion served by people at the front of our gathering space. It's a beautiful thing to see lines of people down the aisles, waiting to take communion, and singing songs about Jesus as they are approaching. It's also a beautiful thing to see

people walk to a response table, take the bread, dip it in the bowl, and step aside to spend moments remembering the life, death, and resurrection of Jesus. I love seeing people taking communion and praying alone, friends praying with one another, husbands praying with wives, and parents praying with their children. We prioritize communion weekly in different ways in order to remember Jesus's death and resurrection as a church.

7. **Giving** is also an important component of our gatherings. We call people to give weekly as an act of worship. Giving is a discipleship issue. We encourage them to give at the response tables where they take communion, or online. In the coming chapters, I'll share much more about the way the church uses this corporate giving to foster our shared mission.

8. Because gatherings are far from the only thing our church does, when we speak of our church, we will also speak of **House Churches** and **Ministry Partnerships**. To reinforce the fact that house churches and ministry partnerships are equal parts of our church life, we promote these two pillars weekly and regularly through announcements, interviews, and videos. They are represented holistically whenever we gather, and through all of our communication forums.

9. Finally, we see our **children's ministry** as a vital piece of the church's weekly gathering. Scripture talks often about training our children in the Lord (Deut. 6:5–9), and this was important to Jesus (Matt. 19:13–15). Our children (birth–sixth grade)

are cared for and taught about Jesus in a fun, safe, and creative environment. They also gather with their parents after our sermon to sing, take communion, give, and pray.

We believe our greatest job is to support parents as they raise their kids to love and know and follow Jesus. Since many parents did not grow up with parents who led them to Jesus, we disciple parents to help them understand how to teach their kids about God. We also teach their children things that they may not know how to teach them. And, we teach our parents how to teach their kids the Scriptures. We offer resources throughout the week for parents to have biblical and spiritual discussions with their kids, and have events throughout the year to encourage them in this all-important parenting pursuit.

For all these components to take place, it's important to have a place to gather together. We believe that Sunday gathering spaces are useful and not inherently counter to God's design for the church. Jesus often met with the multitudes on the mountainside (Matt. 14:13–21) and in synagogues, and in homes by the hundreds. And, the early church gathered in the temple courts by the thousands, then Solomon's Colonnade next to the temple (Acts 3–5). After the temple ruler became a follower of Jesus, the church was no longer allowed to gather in the temple courts, so they rented the large lecture hall next door where they continued to gather by the thousands.

As did the early church, and the church throughout the world today, we too meet in larger spaces to collectively worship, pray, and hear God's Word. We intentionally keep our building simple to send the message that the church is not the building. The caution is to not over-prioritize the space. It is totally utilitarian. Space is neutral. Often, whether overtly or subconsciously, the building becomes the goal, the point, the foundation. But the more emphasis we place on the building, the greater difficulty people will have understanding that the church is not a building, it's the people. Our building is simply a tool to accomplish a part of God's mission in his church.

House Churches

The model we see in Scripture for living in community is the house church, which forms the second pillar on which our church is built. New Testament churches gathered in homes, led by an approved and qualified pastor, where they lived out the community modeled and taught by Jesus.

We see several examples of this in Scripture:

- "Give my greetings to the brothers and sisters at Laodicea, and to Nympha and **the church in her house**" (Col. 4:15).

- "Greet Priscilla and Aquila, my co-workers in Christ Jesus…Greet **also the church that meets at their house**" (Rom. 16:3–5).

- "To Apphia our sister and Archippus our fellow soldier—and **to the church that meets in your home**" (Phil. 1:2).

I've spent my entire life in church. I've been involved in all forms of gatherings in smaller expressions of community. I've been a part of all of these, and I've given oversight to them. But, I've never experienced community in the way I have seen through house churches. I often hear people say the same things to me. The blending of the biblical components that encompass house churches offers elements that many people have never experienced. We talk about these biblical and crucial elements in the next chapter.

If someone resists this idea, one of the first things I hear in a disagreeing response to our practice of house churches is that the modern church does not have to follow this model simply because the early church did it that way. In other words, the Scriptural basis for this practice is *descriptive,* not *prescriptive.* I agree with that. We have freedom, in certain areas, to do things beyond the description we see in Scripture. For example, we have liberty regarding our method of taking communion.

However, a basic hermeneutical principle is that we cannot make biblical arguments from silence. I find most church models or methodologies are basing their arguments on silence. "It never said *not* to do this," or, "It never said that we *had* to do it this way." Which means that many people are actually getting their approach to church from someplace beyond Scripture. So, when someone says, "That's not a biblically-prescribed model," or, "The early church wasn't developed enough yet," I say, "What forms the basis of our practice, then? Aren't we better served to follow the model we see in Scripture rather than try to create something on our own?" I also inquire, "Help me understand biblically why you do what you do." Church leaders often can't, or at least they can't describe their practices using biblical structure and nomenclature.

I'm not interested in trying to prove to people my way is right and their way is wrong. As a church, although we are convinced and convicted about this biblical structure, we don't go around preaching that our model is superior. If people want to learn about what we're doing, we'll share what we've learned. But we don't walk around telling people that they should do what we do, or that they shouldn't do what they're doing. There are great things happening in all sorts of different models among the big, beautiful body of Christ.

But, if we are going discuss how to do church, let's do it with our Bibles open and let's see what God has to say about his church. Let's have some foundation other than our opinion. As pastors, the Scripture is the basis for us. Whether a model is prescriptive or descriptive doesn't matter, as long as it's based on the Word. There is much more to be said about house churches—specifically, their biblical support and how to conduct them—which is why I've dedicated an entire chapter to that discussion.

Ministry Partnerships

While it's easy to focus on Sunday gatherings and house churches, ministry partnerships are one of the three equal pillars of Church Project, and we believe they are integral to the overall health of any church. Neglecting this final pillar negates the complete expression of what God has called his body to accomplish.

We see that Jesus and the early church met the needs of the people around them for the purpose of spiritual transformation. We also see the early church respond to material needs so the gospel could continue to spread (Acts 6:1-6). In the early church, widows were neglected and were going hungry. The church's leaders knew that this was contrary to the gospel, which necessitated that these widows be cared for well. These widows were members of the church, and Scripture says we have special obligations to one another in this regard (1 John 3:17). But Christians are also called to care for people outside the church—our neighbors and the lost. We say to our people every week, "Jesus called us to feed the hungry, clothe the naked, give water to the thirsty, and take care of the widow and the orphan" (Matt. 25:31–46; James 1:27). We need these constant reminders that meeting needs is an integral part of following Christ and proclaiming the gospel.

Yet, the church leaders also knew that the ministry of the Word and prayer were primary to their responsibility. They couldn't abandon these tasks in order to care for the widows. So, they appointed deacons to care for the widows. They added structure to meet needs within the body. We attempt to do this very thing through our ministry partnerships. We identify needs, and create partnerships, leaderships, and systems to meet the needs we know of.

We also see the church taking up collections for ministry needs. One example of this is found in 1 Corinthians 16:1–3: "Now concerning the collection for the saints, as I directed the churches of Galatia, so do you also. On the first day of every week each one of you is to put aside and save, as he may prosper, so that no collections be made when I come. When I arrive, whomever you may approve, I will send them with letters to carry your gift to Jerusalem." Here we see the church partnering together to give of their resources to care for others.

As a church, we follow these examples through ministry partnerships, where we serve others and share the gospel. This takes two forms: partnering with others with our lives, and with financial support. With our lives, we give of our time, our effort, and our support. With our resources, we give to meet individual needs, support the great work of specialized ministry partners, and support church plants.

There are incredible ministries in our city, nation, and world doing things our church will never be able to do. We can't be excellent at everything. But, if we partner with these ministries, they'll be stronger. Partnering allows our church to use the gifts and calling of others. It also reduces our administrative responsibilities and costs and gives our people a way to serve immediately. These partnerships can shift the focus away from the church and to the ministry, which models the humility that should be seen among God's people.

At Church Project, we have approximately 30 formal ministry partnerships. We know and love them well, and they know and love us. Our people are joining with them to do incredible work for Jesus in our community, and around the world.

It's important to remember *why* we form ministry partnerships. Not only is it practical and effective, but it's purposeful. When we teach on this topic, we say to our church, "What is the difference between a humanitarian or social organization and a church?" The answer is that a church meets needs to share the gospel, which is exactly what we can do through ministry partnerships.

At times, Jesus would share the gospel without meeting a need, but he would not meet a need without sharing the gospel (Matt. 9:1–8). He cared about people's immediate needs, but he was primarily concerned about their spirit. As a church, we're going to teach the gospel without meeting physical needs at times, but we're not going to meet a physical need without being driven by the gospel and speaking about Jesus. We care deeply about the needs for their body and soul—we care even more deeply about their spiritual and eternal needs. We always do this with grace, love, and gentleness, and as we are representing Jesus when we serve, we want to speak about him if the opportunity arises. We're always going to meet needs, but we always want our serving and sharing and giving to lead to an understanding of the gospel. We form ministry partnerships with others who share this gospel focus and priority.

Some of the principles that guide our approach to ministry partnerships are:

- Pray, wait, and seek the areas in which God is calling us to serve, or has already clearly called us to in Scripture.

- Start with low-hanging fruit in our local community—what are the most basic needs that are not met around us?

- Discover a local Ministry Partner in the areas we sense God's leading, that already has some momentum but needs more resources and volunteers.

- Discern other nations we can serve as well. Join people on the ground, who know the local climate and culture and who are already doing great work. Support them with money, people, trips, and encouragement.

- Look for ministries where you can make a significant impact, rather than those where the effort-to-results ratio may not be high. We like to find smaller- to medium-sized ministries who, if we partner with them, can go to the next level of effectiveness. And, our people will be able to make an impact and be involved with them personally. Aim for ministries in need of both volunteer service and financial contribution. Try to avoid just sending a check, without sending people to partner as well.

- Develop relationships with ministries you can partner with for a long period of time. Longevity has great payoff, and the relationships that are built can lead to great things.

- Partner with a ministry when you have a committed liaison within your church for relationship, accountability, and effectiveness. A liaison is the leader of the ministry in your church, and they serve to connect your church and the ministry partner. This helps the partnership run smoothly and maintains the quality of the relationship.

In short, 1) decide the domain you are called to serve in, 2) discover and vet the Ministry Partner who is right for you, and 3) commit to partner with sending people and finances.

* * *

These are the three pillars we have committed to since our inception as a church, and God has blessed us with incredible growth—for his sake, not ours. It is powerful to gather together as a church each week, it strengthens our body to gather in smaller communities in homes during the week, and it's a joy to serve others through ministry partnerships. This is our structure—how we flesh this out together regularly. In the next chapter, I'll share the guiding biblical values that organically and inherently link these pillars and help them work together effectively.

NOTES

CHAPTER THREE

GUIDING BIBLICAL VALUES

From its inception, Church Project has tirelessly sought to mimic what we see in Scripture. That's why we settled on the three pillars outlined in the last chapter. However, we also wanted to make sure we approached those pillars in the spirit of the New Testament. That is, we wanted to discover what biblical values seemed to be at the heart of Jesus's ministry and the life of the early church. We wanted those values to drive our gatherings, house churches, and ministry partnerships. We adopted four values that would serve as the foundation and motivation of everything we do as a church. As a people, we would be *unashamedly biblical, irreducibly simple, understandably relevant,* and *radically generous.*

Unashamedly Biblical

The Word of God is the driving force of all we do. We seek to mirror the biblical expressions of church we see in Scripture, and we spend time in the Word when we are together—both in our gatherings and in our house churches. We're not ashamed to talk about whatever themes the Bible addresses. Teaching through books of the Bible forces us to do just that. Teaching in this fashion constrains us to discuss whatever God wanted us to know when he intentionally put his words in his Word.

Sadly, it's undeniable that many churches today claim to be a church but are not based on the Word. For us, we have deep convictions that the Word must be our guide. In Colossians 1:24, Paul says, "I'm here to give you the Word in its fullness." Paul also told Timothy to "preach the Word" (2 Tim. 4:2). Everything we do must have the Word in it. We teach out of the Word, we exposit the Word, and we draw application from the Word. Our goal is to give our church the Word, rather than primarily teach topically (Of course, all topical teaching is not bad) or manipulate the Word to support our own ideas.

As pastors and preachers, not only are we teaching people the Word, but we are teaching people how to teach themselves the Word. So, we want people to daily study through books of the Bible so that they will learn the whole counsel of Scripture. But occasionally, people need the Bible to specifically address topics they are dealing with. That's why we occasionally teach topically—so that we can teach people how to be biblically accurate while still being topical.

I'll often teach our people that my job is to *expose* and *explain* the Scriptures. Then, their job is to *approve* that it is true based on the Word, *accept* it as God's Word, and then *apply* it to their lives. Our Sunday gatherings, children's and student's ministries, house churches, and our one-on-one discipleship—all are based on the Word. We also have daily devotions, written by our Discipleship Pastor and based on our Sunday passage, that we send out every day so people can get into the Word on their own. We believe that the Word of

God grows the people of God, so we center our ministry on the Word as much as possible.

Irreducibly Simple

The second defining value for our church, one that has become a hallmark of Church Project, is that we are irreducibly simple. We intentionally avoid designing our church around an attractional model that so often obscures Jesus and instead focuses on people. We think the person of Jesus is attractive on his own and doesn't need to be dressed up, covered up, or apologized for. From our first days as a church, we didn't want to depend on anything attractive or attractional—from the place we gathered to the way we presented everything—and we still don't, because we don't want to distract from the purity of the gospel.

Our understanding of not being attractive comes partly from the view the prophet Isaiah paints of Jesus in chapter 53:2: "He had no beauty or majesty to attract us to Him, nothing in his appearance that we should desire Him." I know, sounds crazy! God intentionally came to earth in the form of a man whose appearance people weren't attracted to. In fact, there was nothing about him that we would be attracted to, either. Maybe that's what God intended when he knit his Son together in the womb, and the Father intentionally designed him to not be physically attractive.

The body of Christ should look like Jesus, so we've been intentionally unattractive to resemble Jesus.

Jesus was simple. His life and ministry—the way he lived and the way he went about making disciples—were irreducibly simple.

I think Jesus was clean. I think he washed his clothes, brushed his teeth and hair, and had good manners. He was kind and a gentleman. He was educated and intelligent. But he wasn't attractive. He wasn't flashy or fancy. There was nothing about him that was attractive, that would cause anyone to be drawn to him by his appearance. I'm very convicted that we shouldn't do anything in our church's style, structure, or presentations to draw people to Jesus—other than display the gospel. If Jesus did not use attractiveness to draw people to Himself, if the sovereign God designed him to not be attractive to people by his appearance, we should follow. Whatever methods Jesus did and didn't use are our guide and boundaries.

Jesus modeled this simplicity in his ministry, and so did the early church. In fact, around Church Project we often employ hypothetical conversations from the early church as a means of filtering our decision-making process. I'll assess decisions by wondering, "Would the early church fathers have this discussion? Would they be concerned about this?" I think often they would (or maybe they are?) wonder why we are discussing such things, focusing on such things, spending our time, money, energy, and prayers on things that are so far from what they did, and what they saw Jesus do. Perhaps they would be pleading with us to get back to the simplicity of gospel and community, and preaching and teaching the Word, and serving one another, and being generous.

People say, "God's the Creator, so he's created us to be creative," and they'll use this type of logic to defend more attractional strategies in church. They might say that Jesus got in a boat to teach, killed a fig tree, or held a kid as an illustration, so we should make everything we do creative as well.

God is creative, but that's just one of his attributes. God is beautiful, but he didn't create his Son beautiful. The body of Christ is the representation of Christ. If God decided to withhold the beauty of Jesus, then we should consider why he did so and what this might mean for our practices in the church. Jesus is very attractive, and he's beautiful—not his appearance, but his nature. We don't need to cover him up. We think that doing church with irreducible simplicity uncovers Jesus. It removes the makeup and the dress, and it just allows Jesus to be seen as he is.

So, how does that play out practically? For one, our appearance is different from many churches. Our appearance of our building, the way we dress, our handouts—all that we do is simple. We do not desire to impress people based on their attraction to lesser things. We deeply desire that the lost be saved, but we're not seeking approval of people. We're letting the gospel itself do that work. The Spirit attracts people to God, and the gospel is the power that saves them and not our beautiful, polished models or strategies.

To be clear, we're not intentionally repelling people. We love and want people. We care deeply about kindness, hospitality, and clarity.

Everything about our building is simple. We began in an old warehouse, and now we gather in a former grocery store. We have unfinished floors and plastic chairs. We have no moving lights or fog or anything like that. Everything is simple—our bulletins are simple, our order of service is simple, and our sermon is simple. One guy who works here, who has spent 25 years traveling and speaking with great effectiveness, told me, "You have the un-sermon sermon." We just exposit the Word and don't make a show of it. I've worked hard to make sure my eloquence or creativity or humor or ingenuity isn't the focus of the conversation when someone walks away. I want to teach effectively, and I prepare, pray, and study to do so, but I'm not trying to impress people with my sermon. These are the kinds of things that make us different in the arena of simplicity.

Jesus commanded the church to "make disciples" and "feed my sheep." That's really what we're called to do. If what we're doing isn't directly helping people become disciples, then we should not need to do it. He didn't. People will always express that everything has some ancillary benefit for discipleship, but at the end of the day we want to have direct impact on discipleship. That's why we are very committed to simplicity.

Understandably Relevant

Third, we are committed to being understandably relevant to all people. Jesus is our model, and he was able to speak to the priest and the prostitute in such a way that they both understood him.

We want to make sure we're not taking our theological ideas and giving them to people in a way they can't grasp. My 30 years of studying the Bible, and my master's and doctoral seminary nomenclature aren't necessarily going to help someone understand God more. Those without the Spirit of God cannot understand the deep things of the Spirit, anyway, regardless of what words we use (1 Cor. 2:14). Even among Christians, Paul wanted to teach people deeper things, but they could not yet understand them (1 Cor. 3:1–2). We don't want to hide truth from people—we want truth revealed to them, which comes by the Spirit of God at work in the hearts of the people. Our role is to make the language and presentation clear and compelling for all to see, and then trust God to do a work in people's hearts. In our church, we have seminary professors and we have homeless drug addicts, and we want to make sure both of them feel like they're hearing from God, understanding the Word, and being challenged and encouraged.

Furthermore, our methodology is simple and understandable to outsiders. We explain what we do and why we do it each week. We avoid unnecessary traditions that may be unusual for people. We explain things that people may not understand—from meditation, to studying the Scriptures, to communion, to the songs we sing. We've done everything we can to remove traditions and language that are not necessary and biblical and that can hinder someone from understanding the good news. At the end of our gathering, we have an avenue for those who want to pray with someone or talk about Jesus, and we clearly explain what happens there. I believe that if an unbeliever gets the courage to walk into a church, they're expecting to experience something different and deeply spiritual, so we should not be ashamed of who we are or what we do. But we should work to make that experience clear and understandable in non-religious language. So, we are spiritual, but not confusing or cryptic. We've intentionally removed any veneer of superficial or confusing religion from our gatherings, and have just made it a place to seek God and understand him more.

Radically Generous

A fourth value of our church is radical generosity. This is related to our simplicity—we say that we practice "simplicity for the sake of generosity." Half of our budget goes outside of the walls of our church—to meet needs and plant churches. We planted with this intention.

We are strategic in our systems and are reductionists in all we do. We "reduce and refine" at the outset of any endeavor, and through the ongoing work we do as a church. We pay attention to this, especially in the largest costs related to our building and staff. I heard years ago that 98 percent of churches keep 97 percent of money in their walls, and most of that is spent on the church building, its staff, and inside programming. Most church budgets I have led, managed, or know of have been at or close to these numbers.

We cut in building costs because we keep our space simple. We don't ever want to be in a position where we are compromising our values or methods in order to pay our bills. For this reason, we also minimize the size of our staff. Most churches our size have three or four times as many staff members as we do, but our structure and systems allow us to accomplish more with fewer people.

 And, maybe especially, our job as pastors is to equip God's people for the work of the ministry. Rather than hiring clergy to do the work, we hire pastors who understand that their calling is to equip those in our body to do the work of the ministry. We hire leaders of leaders, pastors who can discover and develop people to serve.

We have always constrained our spending by our commitment to radical generosity. The structure of our church serves our desire and calling to be radically generous. We are able to have less staff because of the structure of our house churches and ministry partnerships. For example, we don't need administrative assistants or church offices. Our staff is not central. Our building is not central. We are decentralized and not built around a structure. We don't have a phone number for anyone to call, and no receptionist to man our foyer or phones. And our programming is simple—we simply prioritize our pillars.

This means there are things people may have been used to doing in other churches that they won't find at Church Project. This simple model we're talking about requires us to reshape people's thinking about what the church is and isn't, what programs it should and should not provide, and what pastors do and don't do. People have to take more initiative for this to work, but we find that they are willing to and wanting to. And, we teach them what the Scriptures say about church, pastors, and people serving. This causes more buy-in—more commitment from the people. We actually had one guy (who wasn't a believer but had been around our church for a while) say, "You give your people a lot of credit. You're not doing everything for them." And that's true. It's easy to get plugged into our church—you look at a map and find a house church near where you live, and then you just go. We don't add unnecessary steps or hold anyone's hand through the process. We remove administrative barriers and systems, and get people directly connected to other people.

One byproduct of decentralizing our church has been that generosity comes straight from people to people. We are generous as a church through our ministry partnerships. But, we are also generous with one another through our house churches. We read in Acts 2 that the believers in the early church met *one another's* needs. They sold their things and shared with anyone who had need. They also brought their money and laid it at the church leader's feet, submitting their giving to the leadership God called over them. People bring their giving corporately to submit it to the leadership of the church, so that we can corporately do all that we need and are called to do—support pastors, run in-house programs (all of which are set up simply), and give together to our ministry partnerships. The frontline of benevolence happens in the context of house churches.

Most churches I've worked in, if not every one of them, had a fairly bureaucratic process and budget for meeting others' needs. It was typical for a person in need to come into the office, fill out a form, and then meet with a person who gave leadership in the area of benevolence. I would see a single mother come into the office, fill out a form, sit down with an executive pastor she'd never met in her life, and share her story of brokenness. It would often be a story like, "My husband left me, I'm at home taking care of my little kids, and I can't pay my bills." The pastor would ask, "How much do you make, and what's your debt?" She would provide the information and walk away grateful for the help we gave, though a little embarrassed to expose her brokenness to a stranger. But she would likely find herself only a couple of weeks away from being in the same situation again, and had now exhausted her church option.

That just doesn't seem like what I read about in the book of Acts. There, the church knew each other, recognized each other's needs, and lived in continuous community. They met each other's needs—even if they had to sell their own stuff to do it. The church was intimate, personal, pure, and costly. People sacrificed for one another! In the church of thousands, they met each other's needs through the community they lived in by the dozens. That type of generosity increases the commitment and intimacy of the church to one another.

Seeing this type of generosity in Scripture always excited me because I wanted to see that happen in the church in our day! At Church Project, we have created a situation of sharing and generosity by removing a centralized structure, gathering people in community, and allowing the people to care for one another in house churches. We see this happen all of the time. It's one of my favorite things about our church.

For example, a husband and father in our church lost his job and was constantly looking for work. He couldn't pay his bills. The couple mentioned it at house church because we are authentic, share our needs, and pray for one another. The next week when this couple came to house church, there was a sack of money on the table. The group said, "We got together, took up money, and we're paying your rent for the next couple of months." One house church had somebody who needed a car because their car broke down, and they couldn't buy a new car to get to work and take their kids to school. Somebody just gave them a car. We also had an older lady who had been divorced for a long time and who had just been fired from her job at another church. She started coming to our church shortly before she had a surgery—a life-altering surgery—that was going to bankrupt her. Within four weeks, her house church raised almost exactly the significant amount of money that she needed. When they couldn't meet all of the needs, the corporate giving of Church Project stepped in. These are the things happening in our house churches as people are generous to one another.

Another benefit of having needs met within a close community is that people know whether or not those in need are truly in need, or just being lazy and taking advantage of generosity. Paul encouraged the church in this fashion when he cautioned them to discern whether or not a widow was a "widow indeed" (1 Tim. 5:3–5). We believe those in a house church, with guidance from their house church pastor, are able to decipher between those who are truly in need and those who are not. But, we've had little to no experiences where people tried to take advantage of our generosity. Intimate community is a detractor for deceit.

In terms of our church's corporate giving, God has called us to give away 50 percent of our budget. We started our first year with a commitment to give away 10 percent of our finances, increasing incrementally by 10 percent each year until we reached 50 percent. Radical generosity has been one of our greatest joys, and probably our most difficult challenge. But, it has been a distinctive mark that has shaped our church from the outset.

Some incredible stories stick out in my mind. I remember our first global ministry partner who visited with us when we were about six months old as a church. We asked these friends what they needed, and they said they needed a van to get kids to church from a very poor village. We bought them a van on the spot.

One time, while visiting one of our ministry partners in another country, a couple of people from our church took an excursion with me to visit a potential site for a partnership with a school and church. The building where this school and church were meeting was almost collapsing on the kids. I asked them how much a new building would cost, though I knew the approximate amount because we had built other buildings in the country. The pastor told me an accurate number in the tens of thousands, and I told him he'd have the money in a week. We sent it to our partners on the ground, and they began construction immediately.

I met one local Ministry Partner very early on in our partnership. I asked him what he needed. His answer, "I need a truck to deliver our meals to the homeless." I asked him the price, and he said, "It's about $20,000 to buy it and get it ready to serve food." I said, "Okay, here's a check—our church will joyfully buy you the van."

When we met one of our largest ministry partners, the leaders sat on our couch after their former church had just transitioned away from partnership with them. I asked them, "How did your last church partner with you financially?" I wanted to make sure they didn't have gaps left over from this church not continuing their support. They said, "They gave us $250 twice. And we are grateful for that." We said, "We're going to immediately do about 10 times that—every month. Then, we plan to increase that as we are able and meet other needs along the way as you have them. We're doing this so that you can take this thing to another level. We believe in you!" They got tears in their eyes because they were overwhelmed at the support. That ministry was already great, but we had the opportunity to partner with them to help the ministry go to another level. They're changing the world.

I don't say any of this to draw attention to our generosity. I say it as an example of what can happen when the church prioritizes simplicity and generosity that mirrors what we see in the New Testament. At Church Project, we delight in being simple in order to be generous. Collectively, we have the power to really make a difference. If we keep it simple within the walls of our church, then we can give our money to things that will last eternally—meeting needs and sharing the gospel.

*　*　*

These four values drive everything we do, and once they were in place the other dominos began to fall. Our structure allows the pastors to do what God has called us to do: "Equip people to do the work of ministry" (Eph. 4:12). House church pastors, ministry partnerships, a lack of central office, less programming—it all means fewer staff, more people being empowered for ministry, and more money freed up for ministry partnerships.

I often tell church planters to be guided by their values rather than their vision. Our values guide everything we do. Vision is, of course, important. But, it is often intangible and hard to measure. We actually don't know along the way how things will change, or if our vision and dream will be accomplished. Often, people get tired of waiting for the grand vision to ever be accomplished—the great and grand vision that they originally bought into didn't materialize like they thought it would.

But we always know whether or not we have embodied our values. Values are seen immediately and continually. We expressed our values when we had 40, 400, or close to 4,000 people as part of our body. We have always been biblical, simple, relevant, and generous.

Also, you'll be known by your values more than your vision. When people come to our church, they mention our values, not our vision. People immediately know who we are, not what we're hoping to be one day. They say, "I love how biblical you are and that you teach from the Scriptures," or, "I love how simple it is here," or, "It's easy to understand the teaching." Vision can change, or even not be accomplished. But our values don't change, and they're constantly present. They're part of our DNA. Generosity is part of who we are. Simplicity is part of who we are. Biblicity (I'm creating this word) is part of who we are. Relevance is part of who we are.

Not every church will have the exact same values (though, I would say all biblical churches should embrace many of the same values). But, we can all make sure that the values that matter most are embedded in our DNA, and seek to drive the church's mission by these values. I would actually argue that we are guided by our most important values—overtly and intentionally, or not. We all do what we value most. And, people easily intuit what we value most. Our time, money, and focus will go to our values.

NOTES

CHAPTER FOUR

PROFILE OF
A HOUSE CHURCH

W HEN WE FIRST started, and people would visit our church, they would ask, "Where do singles meet?" or, "Where do college students meet?" I would tell them that they meet in a house church. When they asked which one, I would tell them that singles met in all house churches. All ages were spread out across house churches, where we are more than friends—we are family.

A house church is different from a small group. It is small and it's a group, but a house church is a little church. It's different in that it contains more elements of a church than do most small groups. House churches are multi-generational. The leaders of House church are empowered to pastor. In a house church, discipleship, benevolence, discipline, counseling, weddings, funerals, and other ministries occur. It contains more functions of the holistic church than does a small group.

It's my goal in this chapter to show you why house church is a legitimate model in the Bible. I will also offer a profile of a house church at Church Project, so that you can better envision them in the life of your church.

Biblical Defense of House Church

Early on, many people were excited to learn of this model. They would express that this was a longing in their hearts for years, as they studied the Scriptures and loved the church.

But sometimes I found resistance from other pastors regarding our approach to church—particularly house churches. It was somewhat confounding for me, but I think it had to do with how different this model was for them. Part of the difference was nomenclature. *House church* and *house church pastor* were phrases that didn't seem appropriate to some, likely due to an unexpressed protection of the role of clergy. They feared that applying the word *pastor* to some doctor, attorney, engineer, fireman, or whoever, might diminish the role of the pastorate. To some, it seemed to delegitimize the role of a pastor.

I remember one meeting where a pastor sat down with me and, in a frustrated tone, asked what right I had to follow a house church model when everybody else was doing it another way. Why should we change things from a small group and leader, to a house church and pastor? I told him that I was more than willing to discuss our various positions based on Scripture, but he had to go first. I asked him to describe his model and methodology using the Bible as a foundation, and then I would do the same. After being silent for a moment, he said, "I can't argue my position or why yours is wrong from the Bible." I said humbly but confidently, "Okay, I can. Let's open our Bibles. I'll show you from these passages why I believe we should do things this way."

Aside from the biblical example I shared in chapter two,

there are two other biblical reasons we're confident in the practice of house churches. First, we want a pastor available for everyone. Paul told Titus, "The reason I left you in Crete was to straighten out what was unfinished, and to appoint elders in every town as I have directed you" (Titus 1:5). Crete was a mountainous location that made travel difficult. Paul knew that the people needed a pastor available to them within their proximity, or they wouldn't actually have a pastor. I find that many of our structures today inadvertently perpetuate the problem Paul was trying to solve: people not having pastors available to them. Paul wanted people to access spiritual leadership. So today, if the only empowered pastors are the paid clergy, we limit people from being able to have a pastor they know and who knows them. Or, we have to hire so many pastors that we cannot be generous to outside ministry partnerships. And, we limit the opportunity for laypeople with the calling and gifting of a pastor to legitimately pastor and shepherd a small church.

We want a pastor available for everyone. Our desire is to ensure every pastor is qualified according to biblical qualifications and then empower them for ministry. That's why our house church pastors are the front line for counseling, discipline, and benevolence. Some even do weddings and funerals. These guys are laypeople who are high-capacity leaders, and house churches give them a context for exercising their gifts. We ask these great leaders to give oversight to a small church, rather than having them hand out bulletins or park cars (not that these things are unimportant).

The second biblical defense lies in the fact that the church we find in Scripture was immediately global—meaning it wasn't bound to an individual culture. So, God's design for the church can, and should, be applied in many different cultural contexts. House churches were not simply a culturally bound structure necessary in the first century but now obsolete. They were a practice that can be applied throughout all cultures and at all times in history.

Sure, we contextualize many things about the church. Lights versus candles where there is no electricity, speakers where available, words where people can read, etc. The list for contextualization is long. But, we have to stop somewhere short of the full opportunity to contextualize. Some people will argue that everything is contextualized, but we must carefully consider the degree to which we practice contextualization. We contextualize how the gospel is explained and understood, but we must never compromise the integrity of the gospel. The tenets of the gospel are absolute and non-negotiable. Jesus said, "Deny yourselves, take up your cross, and follow me," to a multi-cultured, multi-language audience.

Likewise, there must be some absolutes concerning the practice of the church. If the church is so vital, so important, so central in the mission of Christ—there have to be some absolutes that God uses to define and shape his entire body. Since the church is universal and global, there must be some truths that can be applied everywhere and anywhere. Since we see the model of house churches throughout Scripture, we believe that this model is one that can, and should, be applied to the church regardless of what other facets of the church's ministry may need to be contextualized. Paul traveled from city to city, ministering across cultures, and house churches sprang up, along with larger gatherings throughout the city. This tells us that house churches are not culturally bound, but are actually effective regardless of culture. And, it seems a model worth embracing since we want the gospel to spread with least resistance.

Years ago, well before Church Project existed, I was on a ministry visit to Africa. I met an elderly woman who walked for two hours to get to the gathering of her church, which was a large group of people who sat under a tree, sang songs, listened to the Scriptures, and prayed together. It was beautiful. But, they needed so much more. They needed to talk to one another, discuss Scripture, know each other's needs, and find meaningful ways for loving one another well. I remember thinking that I could not train these people how to do church based on the church models I had experienced up to that point, because the experiences I perpetuated at home weren't transferable to a new culture. This woman needed a church nearby. She needed a house church to disciple her and give her a family. She needed a pastor. She needed people in the community to create a place to wrestle with ideas about God in a conversation with other believers. These beautiful believers needed to minister to one another and meet needs in their village in the name of the gospel. The house church model allows for just that.

Profile of a House Church

There are a number of practices house churches use to create a growing, Christian community that naturally makes disciples. Once embraced, these practices continue to enhance the quality of existing houses churches and foster the spread of new ones as well. Here are essential elements of a house church.

House Churches are cross-generational.

A house church looks more like a family instead of a group of friends who are alike in age and life stage. The early church was made up of multiple generations, where the older were teaching the younger, the more mature in their faith were discipling those who were less mature, the rich were giving to the poor, the younger were challenging and encouraging the older, and so on. Biblically, we see these values in Scripture:

- Don't let anyone look down on you because you are young, but set an example for the believers in speech, in conduct, in love, in faith and in purity (1 Tim. 4:12 NIV).

- Likewise, teach the older women to be reverent in the way they live, not to be slanderers or addicted to much wine, but to teach what is good. Then they can urge the younger women to love their husbands and children, to be self-controlled and pure, to be busy at home, to be kind, and to be subject to their husbands, so that no one will malign the word of God (Titus 2:3–5 NIV).

- But God has put the body together, giving greater honor to the parts that lacked it, so that there should be no division in the body, but that its parts should have equal concern for each other (I Cor. 12:24–25 NIV).

I'll often mention the mentors in my life as I preach. Regularly, people would come to me and ask, "Where can I find a mentor like that in my life?" I would look around a foyer filled with hundreds of people of all different ages and stages of life, and be frustrated that the question could even be asked in that church. Unfortunately, far too often our churches would disassociate the older people from the younger people, because there was no natural context that fostered relationships between generations.

In contrast, a cross-generational house church creates an ongoing environment for mentorship and discipleship to flourish. Older people love the opportunity to be around others who give them life and who want to benefit from their wisdom. Younger people love having some people in their lives who have experience and are interested in walking with them to support and encourage them throughout life.

House Churches are geographic.

In line with Paul's word to Titus, "Appoint elders in every town as I directed you" (Titus 1:5), house churches work best when they are geographically based. This allows people to follow Christ alongside others in their natural community. Even on a purely practical level, people who live in close proximity are more likely to regularly attend a house church, engage with one another outside of weekly house church gatherings, and experience genuine community.

We want to remove the boundaries and barriers of travel, schedule, and proximity that often keep people from consistently engaging in community. We want to see people going to house churches with people whose kids go to school together, who run into one another at their neighborhood grocery store, who can meet together for coffee, take walks together, and hang out as their kids play in the street.

Further, non-geographical communities likely lead to homogenous gatherings of people who are all the same. People's natural proclivity is often toward comfort, so most people will forego a gathering of diverse people in pursuit of a more comfortable homogenous group. This could result in removing the opportunity to practice many of the "one another" commands in Scripture. For example, "Bear with one another's burdens" (Gal. 6:2). People may find some of the burdens of others to be challenging or difficult and find a different group, rather than do the hard work of learning to love people who are different. But when your house church is geographic, you don't get to choose your one another. God chooses those people for you, and he uses them in your life to grow you and places you in their life to grow them. Sanctification happens in marriage—as two different people become one—and sanctification happens in the diverse community of a house church, as different types of people become one as well.

We highly value diversity. Diversity comes in many different forms—generational, socio-economic, racial, and even on the level of spiritual maturity. Each of these aspects make compatibility and unity more difficult for most people. By challenging people to gather based on their geography, we are, in a very real way, aiding people in maturity and selflessness. We are creating context for sanctification.

House Churches are the primary vehicle for community.

Humans are made for community. One of the beautiful things about house churches is that the size of the group prohibits anonymity and encourages solidarity. Life is shared naturally, allowing for biblical community and genuine relationships to form.

1. *First, authenticity is a natural by-product of house churches.* The gospel of Christ frees us to be honest in our sins, since we are not boasting in our works, but in his work on our behalf. People feel free to avoid hiding their sins or their past and are comfortable to talk freely. This is due to the humility and openness of the house church, especially as led and modeled by the house church pastor. (And, it is important to note that this culture

of authenticity is only possible if modeled by the lead pastor.)

2. *House churches are the main environment where people express love for one another.* People should feel more loved in a house church than in any other environment in which they are a part. This is the place where people will be known personally and loved deeply. No matter how big our church gets, a house church will be small enough for everyone to be known. Here, people feel seen, wanted, and crucial to the church. They feel valuable and at home.

3. *Accountability is another trait of houses churches.* Scripture warns about the power of sin, cautions us to guard our hearts, and reminds us to keep a close watch on ourselves. House churches are a gift from God because those involved get extra pairs of eyes on their lives and doctrine. This creates a deliberate process that ensures everyone is known in all areas of life—from church involvement, to marriage and relationships, to spiritual growth, to church discipline.

4. *House churches also enjoy life together.* People in a house church should spend time with one another in real relationships above and beyond the prepared house church format. Relationships should be encouraged and cultivated through sharing meals, spending time in each other's homes, knowing one another's families, and serving each other's needs. People can, and should, even share the mundane rhythms of life like grocery shopping, working out, or tackling chores around the house. Some

even vacation together. Plus, house churches have parties all of the time!

5. *Finally, house churches create intimacy.* House churches should be the place where people are deeply known and where they know others in the same way. No one should feel invisible, isolated, or insecure. Everyone should be encouraged to make each other feel safe and to trust others with their lives. If people are not known deeply in a house church, where will they be known? This is the place where someone doesn't show up, and people notice and contact them. We can't rely on that to happen in a crowd of hundreds, or especially thousands.

The first church moved from 120 people to over 3,000 people in one day! Those 120 went through some intense situations together—namely, the crucifixion and resurrection. After the crucifixion, they had their leaders leave and return to their lives before Christ. Then, Jesus appeared to them in his post-resurrection body. And if this wasn't enough to build a core, the Holy Spirit filled them and anointed them for the mission of sharing the gospel. This created a unity and intimacy unmatched.

Suddenly, 3,000 people showed up in their church in one day! If that happened in most churches today, people would grumble and complain about the new people ruining intimacy and making changes to "my church." But, Jesus added thousands at once to the church. My guess is that he liked and wanted that. He had the right to mess up their church—it is his church, after all!

Most people love the intimacy provided by a smaller group. That's part of our DNA, part of our Imago Dei. But, another part of the DNA God created was a growing congregation.

House churches preserve the intimacy that people crave while still allowing the church as a whole to grow freely.

House Church is the primary point of discipleship.

As with every aspect of the church, house churches aim to produce disciples. All Scripture creates tension—between God's standards for life and the sinful state of humans here on earth. The Sunday sermon reveals truth and creates tension, and ideally introspection and consideration. But often churches have little context for people to discuss, wrestle, and come to some resolution as to what they will do with the text in the sermon. House churches are the opportunity for people to have a safe context to discuss Scripture, ask questions, and wrestle with their response.

Discipleship is dependent on the Word of God, because it is there that Christ is revealed most clearly. Because of the priority of the Scriptures in the life of a believer, the focus of house churches is on the study of Scripture. God says the Scriptures are living and active, able to reveal the heart, and able to train people in godliness and make us wise for salvation (Heb. 4:12; 2 Tim. 3:15–16). House churches seek to uncover and explore the truths contained in Scripture. We dig into the Scriptures themselves, not separate studies about Scriptures. There are appropriate contexts for these studies, and when occasionally our sermon highlights these topics, our house churches will discuss as well. Occasionally, our house church pastor will sense a need to focus on a specific topic that is happening in our cultural context, or in the lives of those in the house church that he leads. But primarily, house churches focus on wrestling with and asking questions of the passage explained in the previous Sunday's sermon.

The purpose of a house church, therefore, is not for

someone to preach another sermon, but to provide a safe environment of mutual growth through guided discussion. Dialogue is created as leaders ask questions addressing real tensions raised through the sermon and the Scriptures. The house church pastor should not be the primary speaker, but the leader and guide of these discussions. And, the pastor helps redirect the discussion toward the Scriptures and gently teaches and corrects when doctrinal deviation inevitably happens.

In addition to discussions about the entire house church and the primary mandate given by Jesus to make disciples, we must be concerned for each individual's spiritual growth. Outside of weekly house church gatherings, there should be one-on-one times where people gather together for the purpose of discipleship. More mature believers should form relationships with less mature believers. New believers should be quickly paired with someone to assist them in their growth, in the same way that we would care for a newborn child. The dream is that everyone should disciple someone else, and be discipled themselves. One of our Church Project pastors has spent a long time developing an excellent resource that our people use in one-on-one discipleship. Your church may have a similar resource, and there are also many resources like this to be found online. Whatever the method, individual discipleship through one-on-one relationships is a must.

House Church is a place of prayer.

Each house church should experience moments of authentic, intimate, and passionate prayer together. These are not simply times for prayer requests, but should include sharing needs, laying hands on those in need, and seeking God for revival on behalf of our families, churches, ministries, cities, and world. House church pastors should help those in their community cultivate intimacy with God through teaching them how to pray daily, and how to pray together regularly as well.

House churches are the frontline for benevolence.

As we've already seen, the early church met one another's needs. They lived in community, were aware of needs, and sacrificially gathered resources to meet these needs. Because house churches are small and intimate, people can more easily see needs, and their intimacy as a group will spur them toward greater generosity. We should share legitimate needs when we pray for one another. As people are generous to meet these needs, intimacy deepens and groups increasingly "have everything in common."

House churches are sensitive and hopeful toward evangelism.

In addition to focusing on community, each house church should be focused on creating an open environment where non-believers will feel welcomed and invited to explore questions about Christ. Every person in a house church should continually and intentionally pray for and invite unchurched and unsaved friends to a house church and to Sunday gatherings, and look for opportunities to share the gospel along the way. The house church pastor should repeatedly focus the group's attention on evangelism in order to direct believers to share the gospel and make disciples. We attempt to create a context in our house churches that makes it easy for people to engage in this mission.

House churches are open groups.

House churches are always open for new people. It would be hard for us to find a scriptural example asking someone to go somewhere else to find genuine community. No one should ever be told that the group is full, and a house church should continue inviting others to join. However, the ideal size for impact in a house church is 12 to 15 adults regularly attending. When a house church is too big to function in a healthy way—or can no longer grow because of their large size—it's time to develop another pastor, develop another host home, and begin a new house church. When a new house church is created, more people have an opportunity to use their gifts to serve, and there is more opportunity for people to gather in community.

* * *

Those are the essential elements of a biblical, effective house church. They are cross-generational communities, located geographically, with a focus on community and discipleship. They prioritize prayer, are sensitive and hopeful toward evangelism, meet needs, and welcome new people. This may be true of many traditional small groups, and of course they do share similarities. But, the major difference between groups and house churches is that house churches function like a little church—holistically encompassing what a church is and does. And, the house church pastor is more than a Bible study leader. He is a pastor, biblically speaking. He is entrusted with the holistic development of this community. The next chapter delves more into this role and how to develop house church pastors.

NOTES

CHAPTER FIVE

OVERVIEW OF A HOUSE CHURCH PASTOR

Earlier, I referred to a conversation with someone not convinced about house churches and house church pastors. One of his primary concerns—and I understand it—had to do with pastoral leadership, especially whether house church pastors were biblically qualified. In this chapter, I'll discuss the roles and responsibilities of a pastor of a house church and provide a paradigm for how to raise up these pastors.

A pastor is a shepherd of a group of people. The Bible says God has called some to be shepherds and some to be overseers (Eph. 4:11–15; 1 Cor. 12:4–11; 1 Peter 5:1–11). We believe that God has created a specific office of pastor and overseer, and he has called and gifted certain leaders to that role. Yet, their function may differ, as some may exercise their role as overseers and others as pastor/shepherds. At Church Project, there are elders of the broader church at large, staff pastors, and pastoral oversight that oversees various house churches.

This provides additional pastoral support and oversight to the house churches, and it also helps maintain our unity as a broader church.

In a typical small group setting, a leader shepherds a group of people, but is not called a pastor. That's okay— admittedly there is nothing unbiblical with this. But why not qualify them as pastors and call them by that title? Either they're not qualified to be a shepherd, or they are qualified. We should empower them with the title that designates the practice and position of a pastor so that they can shepherd their people and not be limited in their role. If they're not qualified to be a pastor, why would we allow them to lead and call them a leader? And, if they are qualified, let's empower them by identifying them as the pastor of the house church.

The role of a pastor is a high calling. It is a privilege to be entrusted by Jesus to lead any church on his behalf. In fact, Scripture teaches that not all should seek the role of a teacher and pastor (James 3:1). With this role comes more accountability from our Father who called pastors to this task. Jesus identified himself as the Good Shepherd, caring for his sheep (John 10:11, 14). We are responsible to resemble him in these ways when we are identified as a shepherd or pastor. Churches in the New Testament had multiple pastors caring for people and leading them to love Jesus, love one another, and love his mission in his world (James 5:14; 1 Peter 5:1). Some pastors served as overseers of the church (i.e., elders), but the major role of all pastors is to be living life together with the people—providing access for all people to a pastor to disciple them and their small church.

A house church pastor is one who has been identified by the elders as a pastor—fulfilling all of the qualifications listed in Timothy and Titus for an elder (1 Tim. 3:1–7; Titus 1:5–9).

A house church pastor has been entrusted by the elders to shepherd a group of people. The title is important, as is the role and responsibility to which this title points. The kind of leader we're discussing in this chapter is indeed a *pastor*, one qualified to deeply and personally care for and disciple individuals within their house church, and create a culture and context for all purposes of church to occur.

Role and Responsibility of a House Church Pastor

There are a number of essential components to being a house church pastor. In this section, I'll discuss the most prominent ones: leadership, teaching, leading discussion, discipleship, pastoral care, meeting needs, discipline, pastoral support, and vision reinforcement.

Leadership

The house church will rise and fall based on the pastor's leadership, because the direction, tone, and atmosphere of a house church will be set through its pastor. Therefore, the house church pastor should passionately pursue the calling of a pastor, grow in spiritual maturity, and lead the people in his church. He is leading individuals to become a body. He is not leading a class, but leading people from different backgrounds, maturity levels, ages, and socio-economic backgrounds, to become a unified body of believers—to become a family. He should care for each individual in his church and create a culture of mutual support among the church's members so that everyone cares for one another. He should also lead the house church to care for those yet to attend—the unchurched and unsaved—and remind his people of the mandate and mission of sharing the gospel.

Teaching and Discussion

The main purpose of the teaching and discussion time is to create conversation over the tension points of the passage of Scripture studied at the previous Sunday Gathering. The house church pastor should prepare by creating questions around the passage that will create discussion leading to clarity of doctrine and life change. And, parts of the passage that are difficult to understand, or are crucial to fundamentals of our faith and doctrine, should be brought before the house church so they will safely wrestle and wonder aloud with their house church. While there will, of course, be needs and opportunities for discussion over unrelated matters brought about through discussion of Scripture, the goal of the house church pastor is to expose the truths of the passage throughout the discussion and give opportunities to understand and personally apply these Scriptural truths.

Discipleship

House church pastors should know their people individually in respect to their salvation, maturity, weaknesses, strengths, and so on. House church pastors should lead those in their house church by providing tools and teaching specifically catered to the needs of the individuals in the house church and giving personal time to the various members of the group.

Pastoral Care

One of the most significant ways house church pastors let their house church know they deeply care for them is by being there for them in significant life events—in times of crisis and celebration. We should be present by showing up, making calls, sending emails or text messages, or any other form that communicates care. We should make our house church aware of these events in one another's lives and lead them to care for one another well. We can do this by watching one another's kids if someone is in the hospital, bringing food in times of need, cleaning someone's house, mowing their yard, or any of a host of other ways we can show care.

People are especially sensitive to God in times of crisis and often either move closer to him or further away. This means that providing care during these times is a primary aspect of biblical discipleship. We might think that it is a menial task when we attend a funeral, take food to a grieving family, or listen as someone shares heartbreaking pain. But, these basic acts can have a life-changing impact, so they should be prioritized by house church pastors.

Meeting Needs

For needs to be met, needs must be known. House churches should be an environment where people feel comfortable sharing their needs and where it is expected that people are open about their needs. When this happens, the house church will be able to respond as able. A house church pastor is responsible for setting the tone and expectation of openness and love in their house church.

House church pastors should, of course, be cautious about those who would abuse this gift of generosity and benevolence. Though rare, if someone is asking or receiving in excess, it should be dealt with privately and deliberately. If not, the culture of generosity of the house church will diminish and adversely affect those in legitimate need.

There will be occasions when legitimate needs are too substantial and cannot be met from within the resources of the house church. When this occurs, the house church pastor should evaluate the legitimacy of the need and bring the situation to an elder who oversees the house church.

Discipline

Sinners will sin, and a house church pastor must correct and call his people to repentance. A pastor who is not willing to lovingly confront sin should not assume the role of a pastor.

The ideal situation for discipline is when the pastor knows and sees signs of the situation early. They can then meet with the person in the house church before the sin becomes fully developed. If repentance is rejected by the house church member, the pastor should follow the protocol from Matthew and invite one or two others into the conversation to lovingly confront and call them to repentance (Matt. 18:15–20).

If the call to repentance is rejected, the house church pastor should involve an elder overseeing their house church to investigate the situation, attempt to call for repentance, and exercise church discipline if necessary. Full church discipline should not be exercised by the house church pastor alone. There must also be great caution to not spread gossip about the person in sin. The wayward individual should feel wanted and welcomed to return after repentance—certainly, they should not feel rejected. Discipline is for the purpose of repentance and restoration, not rejection.

Leadership and Unity Support

The house church pastor is entrusted with great leadership. They are entrusted with this role from the elders of the entire church. Therefore, the house church pastor should work to increase unity, not division. The house church pastor should never be involved in gossip, slander, or bitterness toward the leadership of the broader church. If the house church pastor has issues with other elders, he is responsible to quickly share his concerns with elders and attempt quick resolution. These issues should never be shared with people within the house church. If the house church pastor cannot follow the leadership of the elders, and will be involved in bitterness, gossip, division, or will lead in a direction other than that designed by the leadership of the church, he should communicate this to the leadership and relinquish his position as a house church pastor.

Vision Reinforcement

The house church pastor should intimately know the vision, purpose, values, and mission of the broader church. He should be a frontline representative for the essence of the church. The house church pastor should be the go-to person for questions from those within his house church concerning the overall church. He should lead the charge for the mission of the church and invite others to join the vision—all the while working to unify their group behind the overall mission of the church.

Raising Up a New Pastor

At Church Project, discovering and developing new house church pastors is the way our impact increases and ministry continues beyond the elders. If a group is healthy, most likely it will grow (there are always mitigating circumstances of slow growth in a healthy context). If a house church grows and has only one house church pastor to accommodate their growth, the house church will not be adequately cared for, and will eventually become unhealthy. Preparing the next house church pastor is crucial for health and growth. And, it follows in the model of Jesus with his disciples, Paul with the first missionaries, and the early church with its members.

The highest responsibility of church leadership is choosing and approving other leaders for the church. Church Project takes seriously the calling to shepherd its people. Whoever has been chosen as a house church pastor has been entrusted to represent Christ and his local body, and to replicate the heart and lifestyle of an approved and committed shepherd.

Because of this responsibility, every pastor has to be tested and proven. It takes at minimum about six months for us to discover and develop a new house church pastor—though, in most cases more time is desired in order to know and develop them well.

Apprenticing is a great way to facilitate this training. When Paul trained Timothy, he said, "You know me. You know all about my life, my teachings, my doctrine, my way of life. You know all about me" (2 Tim. 3:10). In the same way, people should know the pastor's life and be able to follow their example. We have a saying: "Pastors beget pastors." Paul, in a sense, *begat* Timothy. It wasn't a formal class training—it was life on life.

We can never entrust a ministry to someone we don't know well. Even being a member on church roll isn't qualification (though we don't have membership in this sense). We must know their level of commitment and consistency before we entrust others to their care. We must know their interaction with others, their gifts, and their leadership. We must know their condition spiritually, theologically, and philosophically. Everyone has to get the DNA of the broader church before they begin leading. The goal is to transfer DNA and values to everyone—from the original leaders on down. Pastoral training in the context of our local church is the best way to infuse everyone with the same DNA.

We vet guys for a long time, and every house church pastor comes from within an existing house church. We've known them, seen their lives, proven their leadership, gotten to know their doctrine, and listened to them teach. Even if someone has come from another church and another position of leadership, we need to know that they know us and believe in what we are doing. After the pastor has been identified by his house church, trained by the existing pastors, and been a part of our mission for a sufficient amount of time, the elders have final approval before appointing him to the role of pastor. Finally, once we have dug into acute ideas of doctrine with them, they are proven and ready.

Then, we have ongoing training with these men. Every other month we have a corporate meeting with all house church pastors. Each house church pastor has a pastor over them who checks on them, cares for them, and is aware of their life. Our staff pastor over house churches also sends training videos and reminders throughout the month.

Preparation will take time, and even once we've invested considerable care, the pastors will still need to grow and mature. We appoint pastors who are not fully ready—just like the disciples weren't. But we make sure they're ready enough. Jesus could've spent 15 more years with his disciples before he commissioned them, and they still would not have been all the way ready. He got them ready enough and then continued to work with them so that they grew and matured once they had been sent.

* * *

The strength of a church rises and falls on the strength of its community, and the strength of our community rises and falls on our house church pastors. This is certainly true at Church Project. Our pastors are men I love, respect, and enjoy. I like them. I want to spend more time with them than I do. I depend on them. They give their lives for the gospel and the church, and we would not exist or be healthy without them. Discovering and developing house church pastors will enrich the life of the staff pastors in every way. Having colleagues— men in the trenches with you—is essential to the overall health of a church's leadership. My colleagues are doctors, firefighters, attorneys, police officers, oil and gas executives— this makes life rich, diverse, and fun. And, these highly capable people feel a great sense of trust and responsibility when given a house church to pastor.

NOTES

CONCLUSION

W<small>E HAVE ONE</small> short life. To be called to pastor on behalf of Christ and his church is a huge and humbling calling. There's nothing more important than this. And when done correctly, there is possibly nothing more difficult than pastoring well.

You may be a pastor who struggles to envision how you can be a part of a great work of God like you've dreamed about and prayed and worked for. You might be in a place that seems broken beyond repair. God might leave us in places like this for a season to cultivate us. He may be proving us—making us wait. He may be doing deep work in us, of which we are not fully aware. He kept me for years in places of preparation. And, of course, he's still preparing me for things I'm not yet aware of.

I don't know what this means for you. I don't know specifically what you're called to do. But I do know this: Jesus has a plan, is preparing us, and won't waste a person who wants to live out his purpose. Jesus has saved me and put his Spirit in me, and now I want to live it fully for him. I want to leverage my calling—including my time. But I also know this means that God may put me in the desert or prison for a season in order to prove, prune, and prepare me. God will probably make us wait longer than we think he should. I know I have foolishly questioned God's stewardship of my time— I've audaciously been angry at God for wasting prime years in my life! Yet, he has been patient with me, and I'm learning to trust his stewardship of my life.

God is generous to record stories of people like this in Scripture whom he used significantly so that we could see their trials and temptations. More importantly, through them, we see God's plan at work in the lives of broken people like you and me. But, as we see in Scripture, from childless Abraham, to Joseph in prison, to David in the sheep fields, there will always come a point where he'll use all of this preparation for the work he's prepared for us. It takes a lot of faith to wait on his plan.

God initiated the conversation and made a promise to Abraham. He was called, but he waited and wandered and wondered how God would carry out this promise. Then he had to learn and suffer from his own mistakes. We'd all love to skip our mistakes, but we often can't skip the proverbial Ishmael. It's through these experiences that God makes us a pastor he can use. Through our own brokenness, he humbles us, causes us to be able to identify with the people we pastor, and teaches us more deeply about his grace.

God initiated Joseph's call with a vision, and then refined him in deeper ways than he could ever have imagined. He was betrayed by those closest to him, lost his hard-earned reputation after being accused as an attempted rapist, and was forgotten by those whose life he saved. But God ultimately fulfilled his intention for Joseph, and the vision he gave to Joseph years before. We can't skip the prison, compromise of our reputation, or sidestep the hurt others will inflict on us. In fact, all of these things actually help us identify more with Jesus. He was betrayed. He was lied about. He was falsely accused. Being a pastor on behalf of Jesus will require that we embrace suffering like Jesus.

David was anointed king, but then he was sent back to the sheep fields. That's where he penned many of the Psalms. That's where he saw the stars in the fields in a way that he wouldn't have seen in the lights of the city and the palace. That's where he had courage to fight the lion and the bear. That's where his integrity was forged—risking his life for insignificant sheep when no one was watching. We can't skip the sheep fields if we want to shepherd on behalf of Jesus.

You may be discouraged in ministry right now, or contemplating walking away, moving to another church, or starting a different ministry. How do you know when to jump or when to stay? How do you know when to risk it all or when to wait? It's hard enough to begin to fully discern the voice of the Spirit. I think it would be dangerous for anyone to give you a formula or prescription as to how to identify his leading. A wise colleague and friend of mine says, "There's much we don't know, but let's start with what we know." So, what we know is that God is faithful. He also rewards and enjoys our faithfulness to him. At the end of the day, we must listen and obey. When God tells us to stay, we stay. When he tells us to go, we go. After all is heard, we trust that God is at work orchestrating our steps to fulfill his plans through his church.

If you are in a season of waiting, don't waste it. Study. Contemplate. Pray. Develop your ecclesiology. Be diligently in the Word. Discern what it actually means to be a pastor and to lead a church, so that when it is time, you're ready. Disciple people. See what it takes to lead people to follow Jesus, to create contexts for community. Do the work of the gospel where you are.

If God calls you, it was not because of your initiative, but by his design and plan. God is very good at fulfilling his own desires. God initiates a call and always completes the work he began. So rest, be at peace, and trust that, in the right time, he will delight to use you. Before you're a pastor, you're a follower of Jesus. As followers of Jesus, we get to know his voice. So what do we do now, while we wait? Well, we serve, we obey, we pray, we study—in whatever context he's placed us. In that way, we cultivate a readiness to respond. Commune with God, seek wise counsel, be open about your fears with the right people, and seek to obey. If the story of Church Project and my personal journey as a pastor furthers those goals, then this time has been worth it. I trust that he continues to use our church—just one of many reflections of his glorious bride—to show the world that he is great. I know he'll use yours as well.

Thank you for giving your life to the greatest endeavor and organism on the planet. I'm humbled that God would allow me to serve him on his behalf in some way. I'm thankful to do it alongside of other godly people who share the same calling. Until we see Jesus face to face, it's a privilege to be in the work together with you. I hope this little book encourages you to pursue ministry with biblical vision and trust in the power of God.

NOTES

APPENDIX A

10 THINGS I'D TELL CHURCH PLANTERS

C HURCH IS COMPLEX because it is a body made up of so many different parts and systems. But a body is simple—it is created, it evolves, it works, and it runs autonomically with the right care and health. The complexity of pastoral ministry can't be discussed briefly, but I've learned a few things about the basics of church planting. If I could only have one quick conversation with a church planter, I would say these things:

1. Grab a team of pastors quickly.

- Find one or two people willing to risk it all with you, and treat them like the staff they hope to be.

- Teaching, worship, and children's ministries are most important when starting a church. If you're limited in the amount of staff you can hire, people you can employ, or people you can even find to lead, then get worship and children covered first. You'll be teaching and overseeing house church pastors initially, anyway, and from there you can begin to raise up more leaders.

2. Build a leadership team of the wisest counsel you can find at the outset.

   - Wise counsel will protect you. You don't know enough to do this without the input from others.

   - Having a plurality of leaders will comfort your church. Let the church know you have this team. They'll be glad to know that wise people are speaking into the church they are trusting their lives to.

   - Find a variety of counsel. Aim high, be specific with the request (tenure/role). Invite them into your decisions and use them to help shape your actions. You'll need different perspectives.

3. Find a space to meet.

   - Philosophically and theologically, the church has no limitations, but everyone is in an actual place.

   - Buildings are amoral. Don't make them immoral by exalting them or by attributing evil to them.

   - Find the best, available, practical, affordable space that is one step ahead of your current needs. Not ideal is ideal. Not ideal will set a culture of gratitude, will keep the focus on the main things, and will instill an ethic of unity. Ideal will create entitlement.

4. Set a schedule.

   - The philosophy of church—your ecclesiology—is actually fleshed out in time and space. Heaven is timeless. Here is not. When do you do what you believe you should do? And practically, does this work for real people?

- What will you do when you gather, and how will it look? These are things you must decide ahead of planting.

5. Base your budget on what you have, not on what you hope to have.

- Wisdom is from God, as well as faith. It's not ungodly or unbiblical to be wise.

- You can't believe your way into money. You can pray for it and please God with what he gives, but you have to make decisions based on what you actually have.

6. Know who you are and don't change.

- You are planting this church because God called you to. If that's not true, get off of the plane before it takes off. And, make sure you're on the right plane. Make sure that this calling is from God and lines up with Scripture. If so, keep after it.

- Be super clear on who you are, what you'll be doing, and how you'll do it.

- Every change is an admission of ignorance, and people are aware of that. People will allow some of this, but not much. Change will always cost you. It will cost you time. It will cost you money. It will cost you energy. It will cost you trust. Every redirection takes a hit on momentum and leader energy—communication, more communication, recommunication—then you lose people's trust because they don't know if you're going to change again.

7. Simplicity is difficult, but simplicity will save you.

- The younger and smaller you are as a church, the less you need to do.

- Major on the things that matter most.

- Do only those primary things with your time, money, and leadership. For us it was Sunday gatherings, house churches, and ministry partnerships.

8. Always say no, and occasionally break this rule.

- Everyone will have an idea, suggestion, passion, and vision, but their thoughts might end up wrecking your calling and dreams. It's a good sign that they have ideas (it means they care), but you need to know how you'll respond beforehand.

- We have a saying that presents an order of response to a suggestion: *Say thank you, say no, say why, say no, say thank you.* People will always have ideas, convictions, and passions that do not line up with what your leadership wants to do or where it wants to go. We have to treat people with grace, dignity, and gratitude, but we have to realize that not everyone is leading in the same direction as the church. When people make suggestions, we often say something like, "Thank you for caring about this church enough to share your idea with us, but we will not be able to do that, and here's why. (It will change our schedule, our budget, our direction—whatever it may be.) So, we're not going to do that, but I'm very thankful that you care enough to suggest this."

- Don't just tell somebody no, but especially don't tell somebody maybe. "Maybe" leads to disappointment that can linger and build over time. Have courage to be kind, clear, and honest.

9. You can't be a pastor if you can't take a punch—get tough quick.

- There are great, great people who will fight for you, and there are mean people who will be mean to you.

- You'll get punched and sucker punched. Every pastor deals with it. It's not personal to only you. I don't know a pastor who hasn't been hurt by people.

- Broken people will do hurtful things.

10. Don't shortcut integrity.

- The opportunities to shortcut integrity will come in many conversations and in a myriad of little decisions.

- The foundation of your church will be built on the integrity of your decisions and behavior.

This list is by no means exhaustive—any church planter has stories from the trenches and wisdom to give. But, these ten truths were essential aspects of what God showed me as I walked through the tough work of church planting, and I hope it will be useful to you as well.

THINGS THAT HAVE SURPRISED ME

HERE ARE A few things that have surprised me in ministry—and have taught me that I'll never stop being surprised.

1. There will never be enough money.

    - The vision will always precede provision.

    - The provision will always fulfill the God-given vision—including its timing.

    - If there is enough money, I'm not giving enough away.

    - God uses limited resources to cause us to tighten our spending.

2. Leadership is a bigger challenge than it should be.

    - Leading staff is tougher than you think it should be.

- Leading volunteer leaders is sometimes easier than leading staff. If I'm stewarding the church's offering to employ someone on behalf of the church, I would expect that the staff person's excellence, passion, and commitment will be higher even than our greatest volunteers. But this is not always the case.

- Great leaders want to serve, but sometimes they respect leadership so much that they will passively submit rather than believe that they are needed or wanted. Great leaders are there—they just have to be discovered and developed.

- I know I can lead, and I know I can lead better than I am currently. The areas in which I need to grow become obvious in leadership. The scary thing about being the leader is that you cannot hide. People know your strengths and weaknesses—you don't have to tell them. There has to be an inherent humility in accepting that you have areas in which you need to grow.

- If I don't have vision, no one will. No matter the great leaders around me, I have to lead them forward.

3. You'll be more committed to this church than anyone else.

- I created an axiom—"In order to justify, people will villify." People will justify their leaving for reasons you would never consider. And, if people want to leave, they'll find a reason on which to base their decision. You don't have to agree or accept it, but that really doesn't matter.

- People will leave more easily than you think they would.

- People will leave you though you've never left them.

- Some people can't stay—they don't have the capacity to work through things.

- It will bother you more than you'd think and more than it should.

- It will cripple your ministry if you don't get to a point of acceptance and peace. This has been my toughest challenge, biggest prayer, and greatest point of growth.

4. My biggest battle is myself. Everything in and about me will be tested:

- My ambition vs. my vision

- My never being satisfied vs. my passion and drive

- My trust in the power and work of the Spirit vs. my trust in my own strength

- My dependence on the Scriptures vs. my own cleverness

- My peace and confidence vs. my identity in the "success" of my church

- My belief in how much God loves me, sees me, and is for me

- My commitment to my church and my belief in my calling

- My insecurities

- My faith in the work of God and his ability to do things

- My marriage
- My commitment to my family

This list could be longer. I've learned so much, and I'm still learning. Every time I think I could not be surprised, I'm reminded that I'm very far from finished. Be encouraged that our very essence as pastors is to help people grow and shepherd them. But we are also sheep, and lists like this one are evidence that we're growing too. We are pastors; our work is to help people grow, to shepherd them. But we are also Christians, and our work is to yield ourselves to God's shepherding work in our lives. As a pastor, you'll always be learning, and you'll always be growing. It will always be painful. But growth is a sign of life, so be encouraged in the growing pains—and keep going and growing!

CPSIA information can be obtained
at www.ICGtesting.com
Printed in the USA
FSHW022039030219
55457FS